Revival Now!®

A Compilation
Of Messages On Revival

by Pastor Bob Nichols

Compassion House Publishing | Fort Worth, Texas

Revival Now!
ISBN.0-9754200-090000
Copyright 2004 by Calvary Cathedral, Inc.
1701 Oakhurst Scenic Drive
Fort Worth, Texas 76111

Contents

Preface

Is it really necessary to publish yet another book on the subject of revival? Hasn't the topic of revival been hashed and re-hashed for many years? Do we really need another revival book tucked away on our bookshelf, collecting dust with the others?

While it is true that many books have been written on the subject, there is still a desperate need for revival in our land. Perhaps one of the reasons we aren't experiencing revival on a grand scale is because our revival books are indeed collecting dust on our bookshelves. It is time once again that we blow the dust off of the subject of revival. The Holy Ghost will not be put on a shelf. He is going to find somebody, some-where through which He can move. Will that person be you?

More than ever before, we must have revival! I believe that God is beginning to stir us up. Many churches and individu-als are beginning to wake up. Revival breakthrough is in the beginning stages. It is happening in small segments of the Christian community. It is not limited to the Charismatic church only. Denominational churches are also beginning to stir. After a long slumber, the church is slowly rolling out of bed and a new day is beginning. The revival of the past is los-ing its flavor. There is a hunger for a new move of God. I am thankful for my last meal, but my stomach is beginning to growl. I am getting hungry for my next meal. God is begin-ning to do something new. Get ready, church! There is about to be a Holy Ghost explosion!

Chapter 1

Red Clay Revival

I can still see the red clay on the tires of those old trucks as they rolled onto the gravel parking lot. The sound of crunching gravel and the cloud of dust are just as vivid in my memory now as it was then. I stood there wondering where they came from until my mother called my brothers and me into the little church in Fort Worth, Texas. I knew that there was no red clay in the city so the trucks had to be coming from elsewhere. Even as a child I knew these were not regular church services.

Our little church had been one of the sleepiest churches in the whole wide world. We had five pastors in four years. I didn't know any differently. I thought that was the way it was supposed to be. But something in my young boy's heart knew that there was more.

Then something unusual happened. After the fifth pastor, an evangelist by the name of Brother Carl Alcorn was invited to come to our sleepy little church. I'll never forget the first Sunday he was there. He was a John Wayne of faith. He came in, stood up tall, and preached a strong gospel. Before the church members could think twice about it, they voted this man in as pastor.

I can still remember the first morning when the tithes and offerings came in. That was back in the day when there wasn't enough to fuss about; it was so meager. He laughed and said, "Just put that in my briefcase and kiss it goodbye because you'll never see it again." A couple of ladies on the front row looked like they were going to faint! I mean they went into total shock.

Brother Alcorn immediately brought change to our church. He didn't waste any time. For instance, we had always had hardwood floors, but one day he announced that we were going to carpet the church. For us, this was a big deal! Before we knew it, the church was carpeted. I mean it was nice carpet. I thought, "What is going on here?"

He said, "If you'll follow me, we'll build a church. If you'll follow me, we're going to see souls saved!" We had never consistently seen souls saved! There might have been an occasional backslider come to church, but they never seemed to make it to the altar. But that was about to change.

I remember riding my bicycle to the church and

watching Pastor Alcorn preach to practically empty pews. He told us things were going to be different and that we were going to build a strong, New Testament church.

Then one day he announced that we were going on the radio! Radio?! We all sat there wide-eyed, mouths open. Man! We hardly had twenty people in the whole audience that day and he was telling us that we were going on the radio? He just kept saying that we are going to reach this city for Christ! You could see the look of disbelief on so many faces. They were thinking, "Our little church, reach the city for Christ?" Boy, everyone shook their heads. They'd never heard things like that before! Sure enough, soon after, we went on the radio and things began to happen. Our church began to wake up. All of a sudden visitors started coming. This explained the red clay on some of the tires. They were coming from way out in the country, because they heard Pastor Alcorn on the radio. They began calling in and getting saved. And then they started coming in on Sunday.

I can still see heads leaning through the window, looking in to see what was going on. They heard the music and the rejoicing. The church was alive and vibrant. It became a place where people were getting saved and families were coming together. Miracles were happening. It was full blown revival! Praise God, all of this started happening because somebody had a burning vision to see it come to pass.

Pastor Alcorn was not only on one local radio station, but he was on XERF, the big one down on the border of Mexico. Things got interesting. We didn't think anybody would come to our church. But, all of a sudden, evangelists began to come. Strong ministries began to come. The top ministers of the day began coming through our small church.

"We are going to put up a gospel tent next door," he said. All summer long, every Sunday night, we'd be out under the gospel tent. I don't know how many times the police came by to try to get us to turn the sound down. I mean it was interesting. The neighborhood became aware that something was different at that church on the corner.

Next he told us we were going to move the tent between two taverns on Hemphill Street. As the drunks would stumble out of the taverns, people from the church would witness to them and bring them into the meetings. Before long the altars were filled with people sobered up by the power of God. Lives were being changed.

I learned from this experience that revival brings change. Some people prefer a church where nothing is going on so that they can hide from change. They want a church where they can slip in and slip out, and be totally unaffected by anything that is happening. I want to be a part of a move of God where people are being saved and lives are being changed for the glory of God!

We need a good old-fashioned red clay revival.

Chapter 2

Personal Revival

I just love new converts. Many times they can be crazy, but I love them. When they get filled with the Spirit, they can be doubly crazy. A new convert would think you were doing them a favor if you locked them in a church and slid food under the door occasionally. They want to come to church all the time. Sunday morning, Sunday night and Wednesday night are not enough for them.

They would go so far as to ask the pastor to start a prayer meeting at two o'clock in the morning! They go to the church on their lunch hour. They want to be around the house of God because it's where they found Jesus and it's where the peace of God is. They are the first to arrive and the last to leave after a service.

When you experience real revival nobody has to beg you to go to church. You can't wait to get there to see people saved, healed and set free. You can't wait to get back to the house of God so you can see the power of God in operation. There is new joy in coming to God's house. The Psalmist said, *"I was glad when they said unto me, 'Let us go into the house of the Lord.'"* Revival brings a new desire and commitment to God's house.

Revival is about returning to our first love. Holy Ghost revival always starts with an individual. It begins with an individual who is hungry for more of God. It is possible to be right in the middle of red-hot, Holy Ghost revival and not experience it yourself. There must be a hunger for personal revival.

Each one of us starts alike. We start so happy and we are so thrilled that we are saved and that our sins are forgiven. Nothing else makes any difference. Over a period of time, however, we tend to lose our fervency for the things of God. So, when we return to our first love, we return to that original fervor. There is a renewed desire to go to church, to read our Bible, to pray and to give. There is a natural desire to praise the Lord, to intercede and to call upon God. Serving God is no longer a chore, but it becomes a joy.

There are times when I like to come to our church auditorium and just sit. Something seems to linger in our auditorium. The presence of God has filled that place so many times. There is an attractive quality in that room that draws you like a magnet. I do not know how to explain it. You cannot sit in there without something stirring in your heart. There is a lingering atmosphere of revival. When you are touched by revival, you are drawn to the house of God.

Another characteristic of personal revival is a renewed love for the Word of God. Your Bible becomes a brand new book. Bible reading is no longer a mechanical exercise but it becomes a lifeline to the presence of God. You experience the power and the energy of the Holy Spirit of God that is in the Word. It is just like striking a match around gasoline; the Word explodes inside of you. The Word becomes more than just head knowledge. It comes alive and begins to transform you. It causes you to have an answer to what the world throws at you. On the day of Pentecost, Peter was able to explain what was going on to those who asked because the Word was alive in Him. He knew exactly what was going on, so he answered them with the Word. He told them what the Word promised, *"This is that which was spoken by the Prophet Joel."* Personal revival causes the Word to live again in your spirit.

Personal revival is perpetual. It is a constant flow. Living in a state of perpetual revival means that we are not dependent upon a series of meetings or a particular evangelist. Revival is a condition of the heart. Because the Holy Spirit dwells in our heart, we have access to the source of revival. You can tap into revival any time you want. Paul and Silas were their own evangelists when they were in prison. In the midnight hour they began to praise the Lord. There was no praise team where they were. Paul and Silas had their own joy. When there isn't an evangelist or revival meetings to stir you up, you have to stir yourself up.

I am telling you that my family, your family; we all need a personal revival! We desperately need it! Until the Word of God becomes the most important book in your house, you need revival. Until prayer is the delight of your life and praise and worship is the joy of your heart, you need revival. Until you are giving your tithes and offerings with hilarious joy, you need revival. So many people are sporadic in church attendance, as if it doesn't make a bit of difference whether they are there or not. We have some people in our *own* church that need to be revived again. They have become careless about church. I know there are those legitimate times when we must miss; I am not legalistic, but if you can be there, you need to get there. Until the house of God becomes a priority in your life, you need revival.

Personal revival produces a greater love for prayer. Don't you love it when you have had a super good prayer time? Oh it feels so good. When revival exploded in our church, there was a renewed interest in prayer. Because of revival fire, our 24-hour prayer ministry was born. More people began to participate in our early-morning prayer services. God was doing a work in the hearts of the people. Communication with God became a priority in so many people's lives. People were praying more, both corporately and privately. Personal revival will breathe life into your prayer closet. Your prayers will be more fervent and effectual, and they will avail much.

Another benefit of personal revival is that there is a renewed sense of divine order in your life. Have you ever tried to drive a car that had both front wheels out of line? If you have any mechanical sensitivity, it will drive you nuts. You will either have to drive a little faster or a little slower. Every bone in your body will vibrate. Every car occasionally needs an alignment. Personal revival gives us a spiritual alignment. Sin and the cares of this world will cause every spiritual bone in your body to vibrate. Revival gets us lined up again. Our minds become clearer and our lives become simpler. Revival gets our spirit, body, and mind in proper alignment once again.

Personal revival will cause you to be in a state of readiness. You won't need the praise and worship team to prime your pump. Your spirit will be constantly ready to enter His gates with thanksgiving and into his courts with praise. You won't continually need to be propped up and bailed out by your pastor. Your life will be ablaze with revival fire. Prayer will be easy, praise will be easy, witnessing will be easy, giving will be easy—the joy of your salvation will be restored. Cry out to God, stir yourself up, and watch God show up. Before you know it, you will be in the midst of personal revival.

Chapter 3

A Little Post Office On Berry Street

Back in my younger days, God let me apprentice for nine years as an associate minister with my father-in-law, J.C. Thompson. So many people think that "ministry" is just preaching, but I did everything you could do in the ministry. I repaired the roof. I mowed. I even scrubbed the toilets. After nine years of apprenticeship under my father-in-law, it seemed that it was time for us to go and do something on our own. My wife and I were seriously getting ready to move to Austin; but before we could leave, God sent to us Dr. Kenneth E. Hagin who told us, "If you go now, you will be in God's *permissive* will. But if you wait, you will have God's *perfect* will."

God's perfect will for us was revealed in 1964. God told us to start a church in an abandoned post office building on West Berry Street in Fort Worth, Texas. Although we had no money and no people other than my mother, my wife, Joy, and my oldest daughter Susan, we did have a word from God. God spoke Isaiah 41:10 to my heart. *"Fear thou not; for I am with thee: be not dismayed; for I am thy God. I will strengthen thee; I will help thee; yea, I will uphold thee with the right hand of my righteousness."*

You may not have anything in the bank. You may not have anything going for you. You may not have anyone that believes in you, but if a Word from God like Isaiah 41:10 has been made *rhema* to your spirit, hell cannot stop you!

We worked almost day and night to revamp that old building. Back then it didn't seem like God would send the right offerings at the right time, but we always made it. I have since discovered that God is always right on time. After five years, we had grown to about one hundred and twenty people on a good Sunday. I was thrilled with that number, but I knew what God had spoken to my heart. It was much bigger than what I was experiencing at that time, so I was longing for more.

I remember one particular Sunday morning when half of the people did not show up. Half of the teachers did not show up. I wondered why I even showed up. I gave an altar call, but no one responded. After the service, I went to my study and fell on my face before God and I said, "God, this is not why we started a church and this is not why we have worked day and night for five years. I am thankful for everything that you have done, but God, I will do anything that is right and anything that works to build a New Testament church for the glory of God. I want to see people saved. I want to see people coming to Jesus."

Some people are content just to have a "bless me" club rather than reaching out to win souls. You will never go any deeper than when you win a soul to Jesus. My heart was crying out. Although some good things were happening, I was hungry to see so much more. I was (and still am) hungry to see a harvest of souls! I cried out, "God, I cannot live any longer without it! I must see a breakthrough!" That may seem simple or crude to some, but until you come to that point, nothing is going to change your life. Until you come to the point where you cannot handle where you are anymore, you will stay there. As I say to ministers all the time, as long as you can live without revival, you will.

There comes a time when it doesn't make any difference what you drive, where you live, or how much money you have in your pocket. Those things are not important. There is something in the heart of every true called man or woman of God that makes them yearn to have, to do, to see, and to be in the will of God for their lives. I was no longer satisfied with just conducting a church meeting every Sunday. I was tired of just coming together and patting each other on the back. I cried out to God, "God, something has got to change! I refuse to go on like this any longer!"

It was just a few days later that God answered my prayer. At that time, there were revival meetings that were being held at another church in the city. Ragged young men and women out of the hippie movement were being gloriously born again. After a while, the pastor of the church where the meetings were being held decided to end the revival. Too many "money people" in his church were being offended because of the appearance and lifestyle of the hippies. So some of the leaders of this revival came to me and asked if they could continue the meetings in our church. I looked at them and I started to say *no* because they did not look the way I looked. They did not fit the mold. If God ever dealt with me, He dealt with me then! He repeated my very own words back to me, *"Anything that works and anything that is right?"* I told the young men that we would try it for a week. However, one week turned into thirteen weeks!

All of a sudden, seats that had previously been vacant were filled every night with young people. The ones who were already saved were bringing their friends to Jesus. Some even brought their dogs. It was wild. They would park their Volkswagens outside and bring their dogs in with them. Some of them came barefooted. One night I was looking at these young people and I thought, "Oh God, this is not the way that I have seen it in church before."

In a real move of God you will see things that you have never seen before. I would rather see them come in bare-footed and get saved, than see them come in perfectly dressed but walk out without knowing Jesus. I cannot tell you what happened in my heart night after night. If you have a passion for souls and all of a sudden every night you are seeing souls saved, there is nothing else like it! It will spoil you. Nothing less will do!

We raised thousands and thousands of dollars. We hired city transit buses and went into high schools and junior highs. In 1970 there was more liberty to take the gospel into the public schools; so every day we would go to the high schools and sing Jesus music. We could not preach *per se,* but we could sing Jesus music and tell them about the "real cool happening" that would be taking place that night on West Berry Street. We chartered city buses to bring students in every night. Our church invested a lot of money in order to bus the young people in. But you know what? Every time we sent a bus out for souls, the Holy Ghost paid the bills. **Real revival doesn't cost; it pays.** We spent thousands of dollars chartering city buses. If I remember correctly, sixteen junior and senior high schools were impacted by God. We brought in one or two bus loads a night. It was a sight to behold.

Many strange things happened during this revival. One night an usher told me that there was an electrical fire in the building. Before I could go check it out, one of the young people told me it wasn't an electrical fire, but it was a hippie smoking a joint in the back of the auditorium. So we made the young person put it out. At least there was some fire in our church. It's funny now, but it was pretty strange back then.

We had never had drums in our church before then. We had never had electric guitars in our church. Some of the members of our congregation began to make comments about how these young people looked. They weren't as clean as some would like. They didn't smell as nice as some would like. All of a sudden favorite seats were not sacred seats. Members of the church had to come early to get their favorite seats. When these young people came into our church, I heard nitpicking about how they left handprints on the walls of the hallway. Lord help us! The Bible says in Proverbs 14:4, "*Where no oxen are, the crib is clean.*" Thank God we were seeing some activity! Something rose up in me and I asked them, "Would you rather have handprints on the hallways of our church, or handprints on the hallways of hell?!"

I remember one young man in particular that came in. He was wearing cut-offs, no shirt, and his hair was below his hindquarters. His teeth looked as if he had not touched a toothbrush for two years. He had spent quite some time hitchhiking from coast to coast getting mixed up in the drug culture. He was a Baptist preacher's son. He came into one of the revival services and was born again and filled with the Spirit. I can still see him clearly in my mind. After his conversion, he decided that he was going to copy the Bible word for word beginning with the book of Genesis. Some might question the effectiveness of that, but during this process, God gave him his mind back. Prior to that, he could not even put sentences together or think coherently. Thank God, the power of the gospel of Jesus Christ touched his life, and he became one of the most powerful workers that this church has ever had. He reached many other young people for Jesus.

So every night we saw that little chapel jam-packed. Those young people came in and sat on the floor, on the platform, or wherever they could find a seat. They were different. We started seeing people coming to Jesus every time the doors were open. As a result of that revival, not only did many hippies come to know Jesus, but the revival fire began to burn within our congregation as well. Our church was never the same again.

God, wake us up! All that matters is Jesus and reaching people for Jesus! It doesn't matter what walk of life someone comes from, or what kind of car they drive, or what size house they live in. It doesn't matter what the color of their skin is. Let's get past those silly things. We must love whoever walks through our doors. They must be welcomed and loved. When we do that, they will come to Jesus and their lives will be supernaturally changed.

Chapter 4

Who Needs Revival?

It is God's will for every believer to experience a mighty moving of the Holy Spirit. Revival is available for anyone who will open their heart and receive it. However, it is not just a one-time event. When it comes to revival, a little is not enough. Revival is a continual process of being filled with the Holy Spirit of God.

The people who don't think they need revival are the ones who need it the most. I was at a convention in Louisville, Kentucky, where a minister's wife testified that she had been backslidden for years without even realizing it. She had not realized that she needed to recommit her life to the Lord. Thank God she eventually recognized her need to repent. It is amazing how many people come to church, even when there is revival, yet they are cold spiritually. We are in a day when the world will suck you dry. It can happen so gradually that you don't even notice it. This world will drain the very life out of you. Only the life and the power of the Holy Spirit of God will keep you ignited.

Many people in the church do not realize they are dying, helpless, sick, and poor. They are not concerned about their spiritual condition because they are still going through the motions of the Christian life. In fact, I have personal knowledge of large ministries who do not see the need for revival. Their cash flow is fine, their programs are happening and the mail is still coming in. They do not realize that they have stopped depending on God and have started trusting in their own abilities. They depended on God's power to get them where they are, but they forgot where the power came from. The power that gets the airliner up to thirty thousand feet is the same power that will keep it there. If you cut off the power, it will go into a dive. It will crash. Charles Finney, in his book *Lectures on Revival,* said that every born again believer needs to be revived every two or three weeks. We should live in perpetual revival.

Joshua 13:1 says, *"And there remaineth yet very much land to be possessed."* Do you really believe that you have all of God that you need? Are you living as though you don't need more of God? Are you satisfied with the spiritual condition that you are in? As for me, I know I need more of God. I don't have all of God that I want or need. None of us are so spiritually mature, and so full of the Holy Ghost, that we do not need anything more from God.

As a pastor, I have observed a complacent attitude in many people. They are satisfied with the level of revival that they are experiencing because it is meeting their present needs. But one of the main reasons that we need revival is for the benefit of others. We need to experience revival until there is an overflow. It is in the overflow that people are healed. It is in the overflow that devils are cast out. It is in the overflow that the oppressed are set free. You can only minister out of your overflow.

The Bible said, *"Do good unto all men, especially those that are of the household of faith."* It's time to love one another, help one another, and pray for one another. It's time to lift up one another's hands. I need you and you need me. Jesus said, *"The Spirit of the Lord God is upon me; because the Lord hath anointed me!"* What was He anointed to do? Was the anointing for Himself or for others? He was anointed to heal and to set the captives free from bondage. Our personal state of revival has a direct impact on the level of revival in others. How long do we need revival? As long as one marriage is in trouble, we need revival. As long as one teenager is rebellious, we need revival. As long as there are moral problems in the ministry, we need revival. Our world needs us to be in continual revival.

We must be careful not to degenerate into "half gospel" people. We are facing a world that is more ungodly than it has ever been, and only the power of God will equip us to face the things that are ahead. I want to challenge you to continue to pursue revival. Even if you have experienced revival in the past, don't be tempted to coast because things are going so well. You need, I need, our families need, our churches need, our cities need, and our country needs a book of Acts revival more today than at any other time in history.

Was there a time in your life when you were more on fire for God? If so, then you need revival. Was there a time in your life when God was more important to you than anything else? If so, then you need revival. If you have to keep checking your watch during a service, you need revival. If you can write out your "to do" list for the next week during the service, you need revival. It is time for us to wake up. America is not going to be saved by spiritual mediocrity. I am not trying to condemn you, but we must reset our priorities. People are going to be impacted by righteous fanaticism, not lukewarm Christianity.

Before revival impacted our church in 1993, our church was a good church. The people loved God, attendance was good, and from all outward appearances most people would have been satisfied with what we had accomplished. But I was not satisfied. I know this may sound absurd, but there were many times I felt like quitting.

Satan came to me time and time again. He would tell me that the spirit of revival that we had experienced was dying. He would tell me that we were going to lose what God had done. But I had too much of a pastor's heart to walk away. Sometimes we think that it would be easier to quit and start over somewhere else. But God wouldn't let me quit. God was saying, "Let me do it again, here."

I am hungry for more of God! I am hungry for revival! I am hungry to see the people that I pastor on fire for God again. I am going to lead the charge by grace. It begins with me. It is not too late for revival.

Who needs revival? We ALL need revival. Lord, I want to see Your glory fill the earth! But please God, let it begin with me!

Revival Now!

Chapter 5

A Summer
of Revival

In 1993, there were two verses that were so strong on my heart, and these verses still burn within me to this day. The first verse was Psalms 85:6 which says, *"Wilt thou not revive us again: that thy people may rejoice in thee?"* Do you see that word "again"? That means that it had happened before. I knew God had moved in our church in the past, but I had a cry rising in my spirit. My passionate prayer was, "Oh Lord, revive us again! I know You are able. You have done it before, but Lord we need a fresh touch."

The second verse was Acts 3:19 which says, *"Repent ye therefore, and be converted, that your sins may be blotted out, when the times of refreshing shall come from the presence of the Lord."* I knew we needed the refreshing that comes from the presence of the Lord. We needed to be changed. We needed a fresh wind of His Holy Spirit. So I began to cry out. When you get serious with God, God will get serious with you. It was time for us to make room for the anointing and the refreshing of the Holy Spirit. So as these verses rolled over and over in my spirit, I continued to cry out to the Lord.

In February of that year, God sent Dr. Kenneth E. Hagin to minister at our church. He and his team ministered for several nights. Those services began to usher in a new stirring of the Holy Spirit in our hearts. It was the beginning of the rain. Brother Hagin sowed faithfully into my life and ministry for many years. He was the first guest minister to speak at our church on Berry Street. It was very fitting that God used him to begin what would become our summer of revival.

A few months later, I saw a man speaking on Christian television. I knew this man very well. He was talking about a revival explosion that was taking place in Lakeland, Florida. He said that an evangelist from South Africa named Rodney Howard-Browne was conducting the meetings. God spoke to me right then and said, "You are to have that evangelist in your church." I do not say this carelessly or recklessly, but God told me, "You are going to have a summer of revival." A few days later, He again said, "You are to have that man in your church." Well, anyone that has any common sense would realize that if someone is going to come minister in your church, you had better find out something about him. So I flew to Lakeland, Florida.

I was not in the best condition when I arrived at the church. It was very noisy and I had a headache. People all over the place were laughing. All the laughter was very distracting and I wanted to hear what the evangelist was saying. I was not just interested in manifestations. I wanted to know that this move was based on the Word of God. It was not what I was used to, but I decided to wait and see what would come of it all. About halfway through the service, the altar call was given and I saw about a hundred and thirty people come to Jesus. My spiritual antennas went straight up in the air! Suddenly, I began to understand what God had been speaking to my heart.

As a pastor, I have to see fruit. For me, souls have always been the bottom line. I need to see measurable fruit. I am not just interested in people getting a giddy feeling or some kind of fleshly release. When I saw those souls coming to Jesus, I knew that was what our church needed. The following day, I had lunch with the evangelist and I invited him to Fort Worth. He was not looking for places to minister. He already had a stack of invitations. He looked at me, as only he can, and said, "Why should I come to Fort Worth?" I said, "If you can have a revival in

Fort Worth, you can have a revival anywhere." I think that response aggravated him enough to get him to come. Summertime was getting close so we didn't have much time to prepare for the meetings.

In the month of June, Evangelist Rodney Howard-Browne started a meeting at our church. At first we thought these meetings might last for only a week or two. But they went on for five weeks! After the fifth week, Rodney had another commitment so we broke up the meeting for thirty days. He returned for one week in August. When he returned it was as if the meetings had never stopped. The spirit of revival continued to flow. We literally had a summer of revival, just as God said. Our services ran from ten in the morning until two or two-thirty in the afternoon. I would have never believed that it could happen that way, not in America. I didn't think people would ever come to church on a weekday morning, but they did. Every morning people came and soaked in the presence of God. Then they came to the night service that started at seven and stayed until after midnight.

As the meetings progressed, I began to call people and invite them to church. I knew something was happening and I wanted everyone to experience the presence of God like we were. One day I called a good minister friend and told him that something was happening at the church. At first he said, "Brother, I'm busy." That is something that we have all said, but you can get too busy and miss what God has for you. I leaned on him and told him he was going to come! I told him to make sure he stayed until the service was completely over because things didn't really start to get interesting until about ten or ten-thirty. He decided to come and God touched his life in a supernatural way. Now he goes all over the country singing and sharing about the change that took place in his life during that summer.

It would take volumes to describe to you everything that took place in those meetings. Thousands of souls were saved. In two services alone, we had over 1,200 people baptized in water. In one service there were over two hundred different ministries represented. At the conclusion of the meetings, the records showed over 1,500 ministries that were touched by the revival. God showed up in a big way! People were healed, set free from bondages and filled with joy. Many lives were changed forever by the power of God.

Revival changed our church right from the start. Before revival we had a good church, but God wanted us to have a better church. There was no serious trouble in our church. We could have made it, or so we thought. But God had a better idea. That summer we did not have a Singles' service, a Youth service or a Ladies' meeting. We did not have anything except a move of the Holy Ghost. I will rearrange anything to please God. I will rearrange anything to have revival. We will sacrifice anything to do what God has called us to do.

Once again God had sent revival to us and it was wonderful, but it didn't end there. Revival is not a one-time
event; it is the moving of the Spirit of God. I am thankful
for all God did in 1993. I am thankful for that summer of
revival and all He has done since then. The spirit of
revival still burns in our hearts. But you know what? I'm
still a hungry pastor. We haven't seen all God wants to do
in our lives.

Chapter 6

Divine
Frustration

One of the first indications that revival is needed is a sense
of utter frustration. You could call it a holy dissatisfaction.
As long as you are satisfied with the results you are getting, that is all you will get. I'm not saying that we should-
n't be thankful for the results that we are getting, but there
comes a time when we must move to a new level. However,
the average church knows how to make it if God does not
show up. Many things that go on in church services could
go on even if there wasn't a Holy Ghost. Some pastors feel
like they do not need the Holy Ghost because they have
plenty of notes, programs and plans. They rely on their

own abilities to motivate everyone to be enthusiastic.

Before revival comes, God begins to stir us up like the mother eagle stirs up the nest. She begins to remove the padding from the nest so that the eaglets will be uncomfortable. She wants them to fly. Sometimes the precursor of revival is a sense of boredom and frustration. People who get frustrated start reaching out to God. Jesus said, *"They that hunger and thirst after righteousness shall be filled."* Out of our frustration comes hunger.

When I think of hungering and thirsting after righteousness, I picture a man who has not had water or food for many days. He is dehydrated and he is starving to death. Don't you think a starving man is going to be desperate? If he even thinks he sees a morsel of food, he is going to go after it! You had better not get in his way. Would he pass up an oasis in the desert? No way! He is parched from thirst and he is starving. He will do whatever it takes to find food and water. He is on a life or death quest. He will take anything he can get.

"The full soul loatheth an honeycomb; but to the hungry soul every bitter thing is sweet."

Proverbs 27:7

It is popular in revival circles to say that we are

hungry for God, but are we really hungry? It is one thing to say it, but it is another thing to do something about that hunger. Nothing has ever moved for me until I became like a man who was in the desert with no water. You may be thinking, "Come on preacher, aren't you are getting a little too serious about it?" That depends on how serious you are about your need. If there are no pressing needs in your life, you may not feel an urgency to seek God. There comes a time in life where there are needs so pressing that all you can do is seek God. Perhaps you have read every book seeking an answer, but there is no answer that will suffice like an answer from God. When God answers you, it will be like water to a parched man.

When our church began to experience revival, I remember seeing people come to the meetings every night who previously were sporadic in their attendance. They would come and stay for four hours in the morning and five hours at night. Many of them became so hungry that they used vacation time and sick-leave in order to be in the services. Some of them even forfeited wages because they were so hungry. Revival was all that mattered. They were hungry.

Hunger for God comes down to focusing on the things of God. God becomes your focal point. In Matthew 9, the woman with the issue of blood had a single focus—to touch Jesus.

"For she said within herself, If I may but touch his garment, I shall be whole."

Matthew 9:21

She pressed through with every ounce of strength in that little frail body. You could not talk this woman out of it. She was locked in. She was focused.

The blind man in Mark 10 had the same focused attitude as the woman with the issue of blood. He pressed in:

"And many charged him that he should hold his peace: but he cried the more a great deal, Thou son of David, have mercy on me."

Mark 10:48

No matter what the people told him, no matter who tried to stop him, he would not be denied. The more they told him to be quiet, the louder he got. It is not enough to be hungry, but you have to focus that hunger. Revival focuses on the One that can meet your need.

One way is to begin to surround yourselves with revival materials. Listen to revival music, read revival books, listen to revival messages, watch revival videos, and get into the house of God as often as you possibly can. Begin talking to people who have experienced personal revival.

"Then they that feared the Lord spake often one to another... and a book of remembrance was written,"

Malachi 3:16

When it comes to the living water, you have to be thirsty enough to come unto Him. He did not tell us just to go to church. Jesus said, "Come unto me."

"...If any man thirst, let him come unto me, and drink. He that believeth on me, as the scripture hath said, out of his belly shall flow rivers of living water."

John 7:37-38

Some people still do not realize what church is all about. It is not about who preaches or who sings. Church is all about drinking of the presence of God. The world will go to a bar and get plastered. They will act silly and embarrass themselves. They won't even be ashamed about how foolish they act. In fact, many times they will brag about it. But so many people will go to church where the Holy Ghost is flowing like a mighty river, and they will just sit there like they are channel surfing! They will not get involved because they are afraid of looking foolish. You need to drink when you go to church. We drink when we give tithes and offerings. We drink when we praise and worship. We drink when we lift up holy hands without wrath. We drink when we observe the Lord's Supper. Take advantage of every opportunity to drink of the sweet things of God.

Why do people go to a bar? They go there to drink. The purpose of the bar is to serve drinks. It is strange for people to go to a bar and not drink. In the same way, it should be strange to go to church if you do not plan to drink. Do you go to church to be a spectator or do you go to drink? I don't believe that this idea is irreverent. Jesus himself said, *"Come unto Me and drink."*

The Bible is full of references to the old and the new wine. If you drink enough of the old wine you will hurt yourself and somebody else. So many times you hear about crimes that are committed because someone was drunk. Being drunk on the old wine brings hurt. But you cannot overdose on the new wine of the Holy Ghost. The new wine won't get you into trouble. It won't cause hurt. In fact, the new wine will bring healing and peace not only for yourself, but for others. Drinking of the things of God causes you to walk in greater purity.

People get free when they get a little under the influence. You know what happened in our church? We got free from cares. When people began to drink, we didn't have as much counseling to do. People got free from cares, stress and burnout. There is nothing that will take care of your stress and burnout like a good dose of the Holy Ghost. We got free from the fear of man. These are some of the results of hungering and thirsting.

I am still hungering and pressing toward the mark of seeing greater New Testament revival. When you get hungrier for God than you are for water to drink and food to eat, that is when the Spirit of God will move in a supernatural way.

Chapter 7

A Good Housecleaning

There is nothing like a good housecleaning. I remember my mother used to do spring cleaning. I never saw a broom move so fast in all of my life. The dust would fly everywhere. She would put something around her head and then get with it. She was serious. Rugs were hanging outside on the clothesline, mattresses were out in the back yard, and everything that had a handle on it was busy.

So many times when we talk about repentance, people immediately assume that we are talking about those who are unsaved. But really, every believer needs to do some housecleaning. When my mother did the spring housecleaning, she didn't just do it once. She did it every spring. It had to be done again, and again, and again. So many people say, "I have already experienced revival." But we all need revival again, and again, and again.

"So repent (change your mind and purpose); turn around and return [to God], that your sins may be erased (blotted out, wiped clean), that times of refreshing (of recovering from the effects of heat, of reviving with fresh air) may come from the presence of the Lord;"

Acts 3:19 (AMP)

Repentance is part of revival. There is no genuine revival without genuine repentance. As a pastor, I have to be blunt when I teach about living holy. God commands us to sleep in the right bed, and to drink the right thing. He commands us to be careful what our eyes watch. You cannot play on Satan's turf and have God's blessing. Without a doubt, God is calling for purity.

I have a word for young ladies—your body belongs to you. Don't let a man do anything to your body that is contrary to decency, purity, and God's Word. No matter what he says, keep yourself pure. Your body is the temple of the Holy Ghost. Did I make it plain enough? You might say,

"But he loves me so much." If he loves you, he will not ask you to do anything unrighteous.

There are no shortcuts to the greater blessings of God. We live in an hour of looseness. The grace of God is not a license to sin. It is the power of God that liberates from sin. We are not free *to* sin. We are free *from* sin. Sin will kill you. Sin will take you further than you ever intended to go, and it will cost you more than you ever intended to pay. Sin will hurt you and everyone else. Someone said, "It is my business what I do." No, your sin hurts everybody, ultimately. There is no such thing as one person sinning and others not being affected.

Israel never lost a battle when they were right with God. We can read in Joshua 7, and Joshua 22:20 that Achan caused defeat. God told them not to keep any of the spoils. All the spoils of battle were to belong to the Lord. Anything that was kept would be considered cursed. Achan kept some things and hid them in his tent. Everybody was doing right but Achan. Your sin can rock the boat for everyone. Your sin can stop the flow of finances for you and for your church. You can hinder what God is doing.

Look at the state of things in our land. The problem isn't a political problem. It is a sin problem. The Word of God tells us that every man should know and acknowledge his own sin. God is calling for personal accountability. God is calling us to stop blaming others and to judge ourselves. He tells us to repent and to change our mind and purpose. We must turn around and return to God. I fully believe that in our own lives, homes and churches there can be a response to God that will shake our cities from center to circumference.

I tell you, revival renews the fear of God inside of you. The fear of God is not a matter of being afraid of getting caught by man. It is when you are more concerned about God than man. All some people ever think about is if they will get caught. But even if no one else will find out or know, God knows. He sees everything. When revival touches someone, they will become a God-pleaser, not a man-pleaser.

Two-thirds of the New Testament tells us things we should and should not do. If you think that is legalism, then you would have to say that Paul was a legalist. But we all know that Paul was a grace preacher. Paul tells us that the grace of God appeared unto all men to teach us that we should deny some things. I cannot have everything my flesh wants. You cannot follow the dictates of your flesh or your life will be one wretched mess.

Revival not only produces liberty, it produces purity. If you have already missed it, there is forgiveness for sin. It is not where you have been, but it is where you are going. It is not what you have done, but what you are doing now that counts with God. You can start today to do and be what God has called you to be.

God is dealing with the church to get their soulish realm right - to have a pure heart before God. I believe that God is tired of pettiness, spirits of offense and criticism. You can be born again and yet be a mess. God does not want us to critique everything that goes on in the church. God wants us to come to church expecting to have an encounter with Him. If you are so busy critiquing everything that is going on in a service, you cannot receive from God. Your focus needs to be on God.

Repentance is more than regret. It involves hating what God hates and loving what He loves. If repentance doesn't bring a change in what you do, then it is not real repentance. If this gospel that is preached does not change you, you can make all the noise that you want to make and it is as sounding brass. Repentance involves not only hearing but obeying God's Word. Knowing what is right is different than doing what is right.

Calling for repentance is not the same as condemnation. Conviction has nothing to do with condemnation. True conviction will always draw you toward Jesus. Condemnation says, "You can't get there from here." The Holy Spirit convicts; the devil condemns.

I am not seeing how close to the edge I can live without falling off, or how much grace I can employ and still feel good when I come to church. The cry of my heart is to please God with my mind, my body, my spirit, my eyes, my ears, and with everything that is within me. David prayed, *"Let the words of my mouth, and the meditation of my heart be acceptable in thy sight, oh Lord my strength and my redeemer."* (Psalms 19:14) That is also my prayer. Thirty minutes of pleasure are not worth throwing away the precious blessings of God in your life. God forgives, but you can't afford the downtime; the comeback takes too long. We don't have time to veer off course.

It is not a happy day when you realize that what you are doing is not pleasing to the Lord, but once you have truly repented, you don't need to stay under a load of guilt. When the prodigal son in Luke 15 came home, they had a party. Yes, there needs to be repentance, but when people get right with God, it is time to party. When people repent, there is a release, there is a refreshing, there is a renewing, and there is a renewed joy.

I remember when we would go on vacation, my dad would always take the car in to the mechanic. He would say, "Check it over stem to stern, bumper to bumper. I do not want to take my family on the road with a car that is not running right. Check it out. And see if you can find something that would not be road worthy." He knew the value of regular maintenance. Yes, we are complete in Christ, but we are still growing. We are forgiven. We are saved. We are born again. But we all need a checkup from time to time.

Repentance is a humbling process. I cannot tell you how many times while sitting in a service, God has dealt with me—me, the pastor—about something and I had to make an attitude check, sitting right there in church. When you repent, you change; you turn around. You can talk about repentance all day long, but when you really repent, you will turn around and go a different way. You will return to God, that your sins may be blotted out, and the times of refreshing shall come from the presence of the Lord.

Revival Now!

Chapter 8

Joy Revolution

When God's people lose their joy, it is time for revival. John 15:11 says, *"These things have I spoken unto you, that my joy might remain in you, and that your joy might be full."*

Jesus is doing the talking in this scripture. *"These things have I spoken unto you."* In other words, He is promising us that we can have the same joy that He walked in. Although Jesus promised it, so few have received even a semblance of this fulness of joy. I am talking about supernatural joy. When Jesus proclaimed in that verse that our joy would be complete or full, He used the Greek word *pleroo*. It is a word that describes a house filled with perfume—filled to overflowing. Jesus said, *"As a house filled with fragrant perfume, I want you filled with My overflowing joy."*

Salvation should fill us with joy. The Word of God said in Psalms 51:12 *"Restore unto me the joy of Thy salvation."* David made this statement after he had committed the great sin with Bathsheba. When you miss God, one of the first things to go is your joy. You are on dangerous ground when your joy level is low. You can't run your vehicle without oil and a believer cannot operate without the oil of joy. If you have missed it, you need to call out to the Lord. God will not only restore your joy, He will restore you!

I remember when we were ministering in Brisbane, Australia. We began to frequent a certain coffee shop. One particular day there was a number of us who went there and we were all full of the joy of the Lord. We were given some strange looks as we were going in. We were just enjoying life and experiencing the joy of the Lord. Everyone was watching us, not knowing what to think. Finally, the waitresses came to us and said, "You know, we haven't had a crowd like you in here before!" People's frowns turned into smiles. After going there for two or three days in a row, they would all smile when they saw us coming. They called us "the happy crowd." When we went into the coffee shop, the last day we were there, they said, "Oh! Since you have started coming here this is a different place." Well, that is the way it should be! The presence of God should make any place a different place.

The Bible tells us in Hebrews that Jesus was anointed with the oil of gladness above His fellows. I cannot read that any other way but that Jesus was the happiest man that ever walked the face of this earth! Of course, in the hours of Calvary there was grief and suffering and agony that none of us could ever understand. When He drank of that perverted, filthy, sinful cup it was beyond what anyone could imagine. In the midst of it all He still operated in joy!

"Looking unto Jesus the author and finisher of our faith; who for the joy that was set before him endured the cross, despising the shame, and is set down at the right hand of the throne of God."

Hebrews 12:2

Jesus took the cup of sin that we might have forgiveness and life everlasting. He suffered all of it so that we could have joy.

I marvel at the kind of joy Jesus had. How could He put up with the Pharisees and the Sadducees? Jesus put up with all kinds of religion, but Jesus maintained His joy! The joy He gives is not dependent on pleasant circumstances. It is not dependent on being treated right. In fact, the joy of the Lord will work when no one else is doing what is right.

Some claim that since they have already experienced

"the joy," they don't need any more. One somber-faced preacher said, "We watched a Rodney Howard-Browne video one night and we already experienced the joy." I thought, "If that is true, then notify your face, sir." Someone else said, "I am just afraid I will get too much of that joy." Don't worry about it, honey. If you're so afraid of being too joyful, it probably won't happen to you. But if it does, you will be glad!

Some have asked, "But what about some of the extremes?" What about some of the extreme laughter, the hilarity, the exuberance that some have considered excessive? Well, let me ask about the other side of the coin. What about the extreme sadness, depression, gloom, and backslidden attitudes that are prevalent in churches today? You may ask, "What if people get in the flesh?" Honey, you are already in the flesh. Poke yourself and see if you are still breathing. If you are still breathing, you are in the flesh. You are going to be in the flesh as long as you live. Now the question is, what are you going to let God do with that flesh? The flesh is either going to glorify God or it is going to glorify your old religious self.

Someone said, "I am not into that joy." I thought, "I can tell it by your face!" There is nothing wrong with the joy of the Lord. The truth is that God has joy for you. God has a new touch for you. Church is more than just coming to a building. Church is worshiping Jesus; it is letting the joy of the Lord be your strength. I am a stickler for the Word of

God, but there are so many dry "Word" preachers across the land. We need a revolution of the joy of the Lord. We need a manifestation of joy. Revival is built on the foundation of the Word, but you must let the joy of the Lord be your strength.

Notice the strong Biblical directive in Psalms 32:11, *"Be glad in the Lord..."* That means we are to choose to be glad. *"Be glad in the Lord and rejoice, ye righteous."* Are you born again? Are you the righteousness of God in Christ? We do not teach a sin consciousness, but we do teach that those who are the righteousness of God in Christ need to repent on a regular basis. Likewise, the righteous of God in Christ need to return to the joy of their salvation. God wants the righteous to be glad in the Lord and rejoice.

I remember one old minister who was set in his ways; I mean he was set in concrete. I think that his face would have cracked if he smiled. His son got involved in drugs and alcohol. Satan almost killed that boy! When God set the son free, God set the dad free too! Talk about joy! Both the father and the son have great joy because they have seen the power of the soul set free. There is joy in heaven over every soul that repents! If you saw your family member that had been enslaved in bondages set free and cleansed by the power of God, you would have to be hard-hearted not to get happy about it. You would shout, "Hallelujah! Thank God! Once they were lost but now they are found!"

Israel was delivered out of the bondage of Egypt with great joy. Miriam, Moses' sister, had a tambourine and she began to play and dance and rejoice before the Lord. You may not always feel like praising the Lord. I don't always feel like it either. But it sure beats singing the blues. It sure beats rehearsing all the negative things going on in your life. Just begin to thank God that things are as good as they are and that they are getting better every day. Begin to rejoice. You can have the victory when you rejoice, even when you are in a hard place. The voice of praise is always the voice of victory!

I believe that joy in the Holy Ghost is God's answer to end time pressure, stress, burnout, depression and heaviness. We live in a stressed out world. People are living on the edge. Road rage is a common thing. People are killing others simply because they do not like the way they drive. Even professing believers are stressed out. Thank God that joy in the Holy Ghost is the answer. So many of God's people are under pressure over their schedules. We can be so over-booked that we have no time for the things of God. Joy will set you free from end-time pressure.

Did you know that joy is good for your health? It's been right there in the Bible all along, but now the doctors at the Mayo Clinic have made the same great discovery. They now encourage all their patients to check out funny, old movies like Laurel and Hardy, Lucy and some of those others that make you laugh. Some might think that laughter is not spiritual, but even this world has figured out that it is better to laugh than to be depressed. Depressed people take their life. Depressed people will jump all over you. People who are hurting will hurt somebody else. Happy people are a lot more enjoyable to be around. And so at Mayo Clinic they have discovered that happy people heal faster. Proverbs 17:22 says, *"A merry heart doeth good like a medicine: but a broken spirit drieth the bones."* If you have been wounded, I am telling you how to get healed. Rejoice in the Lord. Get a good dose of joy!

In Acts 20:24 Paul said, *"So that I might finish my course with joy."* Oh, that has been a cry of my heart for years. I do not want to finish my course in sadness, bitterness, or sarcasm. I have seen so many bitter preachers. They have become bitter towards people. People can be cruel, but I refuse to let anyone or anything steal my joy. In ministry you have to develop a tough hide while you keep a tender heart. If someone has wronged you, let it go! Forgive them and watch the joy of the Lord return to your life. I want to finish my course with joy.

Chapter 9

Noise and the Wind

Revival is almost always characterized by emotional excitement. The most exciting place in any city ought to be the house of God. We are not designed to be walking corpses. A church that is in the midst of revival will be full of life and movement. It will become the happiest place in town.

A real Jesus revival is noisy. It is characterized by singing, clapping, shouting, crying, groaning, weeping, and laughing. These noises are offensive to some. Although it is true that God is not hard of hearing, He is also not afraid of loud noise. Religion says that church has to be a quiet and rigid place, but true revival will set you free from dead religion. Many pastors want to pastor a church with dignified, rich, and elite members. It adds a sense of prestige to the image of the church. These pastors feel like a dignified church will influence more people to come to Jesus. They are afraid that loud noise will scare people away. But in reality, nothing influences people like a move of the Holy Ghost.

Many times, our churches attempt to be so sedate, so calm, so dignified, and so acceptable. We do this so that we will not be offensive to anyone. We have to get out of that mentality. The noise of revival will always be offensive to someone. God wants us to be free from religion and from the pressure to please everyone. We are not here to impress anyone but God. When the revival begins to flow, we just need to let the wind blow, get out of the driver's seat, and take our foot off of the brakes. God wants us to come into a new freedom. In the book of Acts, those who were in the Upper Room discovered a sense of freedom and reckless abandon. They were not concerned about the noise level. They were not concerned with what people thought about the manifestations of the Holy Ghost. They were free to take revival to anyone who would accept it. Thank God for freedom!

"And when the day of Pentecost was fully come, they were all with one accord in one place. And suddenly there came a sound from heaven as of a rushing mighty

> *wind, and it filled all the house where they were sitting. And there appeared unto them cloven tongues like as of fire, and it sat upon each of them. And they were all filled with the Holy Ghost, and began to speak with other tongues, as the Spirit gave them utterance."*
>
> **Acts 2:1-4**

The day of Pentecost was noisy. Can you imagine? There was a sound as of a rushing mighty wind! It filled the entire house where they were sitting. That must have been awesome! The wind of revival is an amazing thing. When the wind of God begins to blow, strange and noisy things will begin to happen.

Have you ever been close enough to a tornado that you could hear it? Not only have I been close to a tornado, I have been in one! I have witnessed first hand the kind of damage that strong winds can do. I have seen it up close and personal—too close! On March 28, 2000, our church building in downtown Fort Worth, Texas was devastated by a tornado. In fact, one report said that there may have been twin tornadoes. There were about 100 people in the church building that evening. It was a miracle of God that no one was killed or seriously injured. My wife and I were sitting in my office with a precious couple from our church when one of the security guards came in and told us we needed to get out quickly. We took cover and God spared our lives. After it was over, my office, where we had been only moments before, was transformed into a blender of shattered glass and debris. That wind was deadly! That wind was powerful!

Natural tornadoes strike fear into the hearts of most people. I remember on one occasion, I was preaching in the little town of Duncan, Oklahoma. While I was preaching, a tornado was spotted close by and the tornado sirens sounded. The people in the audience heard the sirens, but I did not. All of a sudden, three-fourths of my audience got up and left. They walked out right in the middle of my message. I thought I had offended them. After the service, I went to the pastor's house. I asked him what I had said that made so many people leave the service. He just roared with laughter and explained to me that I had not heard the tornado siren. I was relieved that it wasn't my preaching. The reason I tell this story is to point out that strong winds, in the natural, can be harmful and frightening. The wind of the Holy Ghost is powerful as well, but it will not hurt you. Instead, it will blow everything out of your way that is not of God. It will deliver you. The wind of the Holy Ghost is the noise of real revival and it brings restoration and healing.

> *"And there appeared unto them cloven
> tongues like as of fire, and it sat upon
> each of them. And they were all filled
> with the Holy Ghost and began to speak
> with other tongues, as the Spirit gave
> them utterance."*
>
> **Acts 2:3-4**

The fire of God began to burn on the day of Pentecost. They began to speak in other tongues. Things were moving and shaking. It was noisy! As a result, multitudes were swept into the Kingdom of God. The result of all the noise was a harvest of souls. Because of the noisy manifestations of the Holy Ghost, all of Jerusalem became conscious of the gospel of Jesus Christ. When excited crowds begin to gather for a specific purpose, there will be noise.

I have been in some services where there is a "holy roar." It is when people begin to lift their voices in prayer and praise and the volume rises to a fever pitch. I remember being in a camp meeting in Tulsa, Oklahoma several years ago, when I experienced one of the greatest moments that I can remember. We began praying in the Spirit and praising God. As we continued to do this, the level of noise began to escalate. This went on for thirty of forty minutes. You cannot manufacture something like that. It was an awesome moment. Only God can orchestrate a situation like that.

Noise is just a by-product of true revival. Excitement brings noise. People get excited and cheer loudly at football games, basketball games, and hockey games. It is not unusual or disturbing to most people at all. It is thought to be a normal response to the excitement of what is taking place. But for some reason, church-goers are expected to sit quietly in the pews, having no expression or emotion. Some people are turned off by the emotion of a true revival. But for every religious skeptic that turns his nose up at revival, there is a desperate soul who is hungry for more of God. The noise is actually attractive to those people. It tells them there is life and hope in the Holy Ghost. I have discovered that when there is greater liberty, there are a greater number of salvations, a greater number of healings, and a greater number of people who get filled with the Holy Ghost.

Many people are concerned that the noise of revival will lead to fanaticism. Well, I would much rather see people who are fanatically alive than fanatically dead. It is much more fun to go with the Holy Ghost. Revival is much more fun than dead religion. I have seen both, and believe me, I like revival much more. You cannot have it both ways. If you really want revival, then you have to be ready for noise. You cannot have a quiet Pentecost.

Heaven will be noisy. It will be full of loud and joyful shouts of praise! If the sounds of revival bother you here on earth, wait until you get to heaven. You haven't seen anything yet!

---

*"And I beheld, and I heard the voice of
many angels round about the throne and
the beasts and the elders: and the number of them was ten thousand times ten
thousand, and thousands of thousands;
Saying with a loud voice, Worthy is the
Lamb that was slain to receive power,
and riches, and wisdom, and strength,
and honor, and glory, and blessing."*

Revelation 5:11-12

Why not experience some of heaven on earth while
the wind of the Spirit is blowing? The noises of revival are
signs of life and health. Our churches don't need noise for
the sake of noise itself; but they don't have to be grave-
yards either. If the Spirit of God is truly in the services,
there will be liberty. I want to welcome the Holy Ghost
into our services. I say, let the fire burn. Let the wind blow.
Let God be God. Do it any way You want to do it, Lord; but
please, do it here!

Chapter 10

Consuming Fire

Matthew 3:11 says, *"I indeed baptize you with water unto repentance: but he that cometh after me is mightier than I, whose shoes I am not worthy to bear: he shall baptize you with the Holy Ghost, and with fire."*

There is something to the fire. Not only does the fire illuminate impurities, it also purifies. We do not need to fear the fire any more than we need to fear the wind of the Holy Spirit. The only things it burns up are the things that bind us. It was a live coal from the altar that purified the tongue of Isaiah the prophet. Fire consumes everything that is not of God. The only thing that the three Hebrew children lost in the fiery furnace was that which bound them! The next time King Nebuchadnezzar looked, they were loose and very much alive.

Real revival destroys everything in its path that is unwilling to change. There were recently some devastating fires that swept parts of the Rocky Mountains where some friends of ours live. Those fires destroyed numerous homes before stopping just over the hill from their house. The heat was so intense that before the fire would even reach the trees in its path, the trees would explode in flames. The fire of God will only destroy the works of the enemy. That same fire motivates, energizes, and empowers those who are hungry for God. I am convinced that no minister will truly be effective until he is touched by the fire. Just as the prophet Jeremiah said, *"His word was in mine heart as a burning fire shut up in my bones."* When we deliver a message with the fire of God in our hearts, lives will not only be touched, they will be changed! God promised Jeremiah that if he would be faithful to preach what He told him, His words would be like fire in his mouth and the people like wood.

"Wherefore thus saith the LORD God of hosts, Because ye speak this word, behold, I will make my words in thy mouth fire, and this people wood, and it shall devour them."
Jeremiah 5:14

One evening during the revival in 1993, several fire

trucks roared up to our church. The firefighter said, "Where is the fire? We have had several calls that there is a fire on the roof of this church." I tried to explain it and then I just gave up. There is no practical way to explain to a firefighter that it is Holy Ghost fire and not a natural, physical fire. They are trained to look for natural fire. They looked all over the building and could not find it. But we found it. We found the true, real fire. We experienced it. It was a sign and a wonder. The fire of God was visible.

So in revival there is a fire that begins to burn in our hearts. When I see the anointing and the fire on other people, I want to experience the same thing. We are in a time when we need each other. If the fire of God is burning in you, then I need you to help keep the fire burning in me.

Acts 2:3 tells us, *"And there appeared unto them cloven tongues like as of fire, and it sat upon each of them."* The people outside on the day of Pentecost asked, "What is this all about?!" Peter, who should have been the least qualified, was used by God to explain what this was. The fire brought boldness. He lifted up his voice. He was not preaching "Peter," he was preaching "Jesus." He was preaching the Word of God. He was preaching with the Holy Ghost and fire. All of a sudden Peter had instant recall on what God had been telling him for three years. Peter, the guy with his foot in his mouth, was changed. Although he had failed so often, he stood up and spoke as an oracle of God. He saw three thousand people born again in one day! If I could give an altar call and see three thousand people come to Jesus, I would go home shouting the high praises of God! That is a good life's work all in one night. He was consumed with the fire of God.

Real revival will gather a crowd. When I was a child, I acted like a child. And when I grew up I thought I was more mature. I should know better, but one day I was driving home and I saw two ambulances and three fire trucks barreling down the road with the sirens blaring. All of a sudden I became a child again. Every shred of maturity in me was suddenly gone. I found myself following right after them. Now please understand me, I don't do that every time I see a fire truck, but we all like to find out where the fire is, don't we? Real fire will draw a crowd. Revival fire will also draw a crowd. I followed those three fire trucks to a neighborhood. There were cars lined up and down the street. People were wanting to see what was going on. I asked someone, "What's on fire?" They said, "A dog house." People just stood there watching, like they have never seen anything burn in their life. Grown people watching firemen put out fire in a dog house? People will go where the fire is.

There are a lot of things that I don't know, but I know the fire. There are some things that you cannot do unless the fire of God is on you. This fire is a passion for Jesus that burns in the heart of a believer. This fire will consume you with zeal for the house of God. The fire will change you. The fire will rearrange your priorities and motivations. The fire will get into your pocketbook. It will get into your conversation and your fellowship. I know some people cannot keep the victory because they keep hanging around gossipy, mouthy, religious people who can always give you the latest gossip but they cannot tell you about the latest move of the Holy Ghost. You need to hang out with people that will build a fire under you.

We need a double dose of the fire of God. We need it in our marriages, in our children, and our grandchildren. That is one of the burning desires of my heart. I do not want my grandchildren to be lukewarm. I want them to be on fire. I want them to know the power of the Holy Spirit of God. The fire of God will consume you until all that makes any difference in your life is having more of Jesus.

Chapter 11

There Is A River

Often you will hear revival referred to as "the river." Someone might ask you, "Are you in the river?" Make no mistake about it, there is a river. This river is of God and it is flowing in the world today bringing change.

A river is always flowing. It is always fresh; it does not get stagnant. Water becomes stagnant when it is allowed to collect and there is no outlet for it to continue to flow. We can be like that spiritually. You will become stale spiritually if you do not allow this river to flow out of you to others. You must minister out of the overflow. That is part of the refreshing process. God fills you up and then pours you out. Then you go back for more and repeat the process. If you stay refreshed, others are refreshed and the revival grows and spreads.

When you look down from an airplane, you can see rivers. It is intriguing to see the rivers from thirty thousand feet in the air. Sometimes you see two or three. You can see those rivers winding; they don't always follow a straight course. **A river will take the path of least resistance.** Likewise, the river of God will flow through those who do not put up a fight. The river is not going to beat you down or run over you. If you do not want the river, the river will just flow right around you and flow on to someone else that is hungry for God.

You must yield to the river of God. The moving of the Spirit of God is a flow, not a force. God is not going to force you into revival. The word "yield" means to give the right of way. It is not a mentality where you throw up your hands in defeat because you cannot fight anymore. It is, however, a conscious decision to "get out of the driver's seat" and allow the Holy Spirit to do His work in your heart. You might laugh, cry or be silent in His presence. When you realize the love that God has for you, and that He desires you to have His best, you will gladly yield to the Holy Spirit.

The soil around the Mississippi River is rich with minerals. It has been said that the soil along the river is so fertile that you could produce enough food to wipe out world hunger. Just from that one river! Now imagine how much life must be flowing from the river of God. Think of the power that is resident in it. The miracles you need for your life are in it. Salvation for your family is there. It is a river of life. Peace and joy are in that river. God has made provision for your every need in His presence, in this river of revival.

People get concerned about excess in the move of God. There will always be those that start doing their own thing and get out of the will of God. But that is no reason for you to stay away from the flow of revival. God always has a plan. There are two banks to every river. The banks keep the river flowing down the right path. In revival these "two banks" are the Word of God and the moving of the Spirit. You cannot successfully have one without the other. Nothing can supersede the Word of God. It is the foundation on which everything else is built. The moving of the Spirit is what breathes life into the Word that is being preached. Someone once said, "Without the Spirit you will dry up and without the Word you will blow up." These two elements bring revival into perfect balance.

"Afterward he brought me again unto the door of the house; and, behold, waters issued out from under the threshold of the house eastward: for the forefront of the house stood toward the east, and the waters came down from under from the right side of the house, at the south side of the altar. Then brought he me out of the way of the gate northward, and led me about the way

> *without unto the utter gate by the way that looketh eastward; and, behold, there ran out waters on the right side. And when the man that had the line in his hand went forth eastward, he measured a thousand cubits, and he brought me through the waters; the waters were to the ankles. Again he measured a thousand, and brought me through the waters; the waters were to the knees. Again he measured a thousand, and brought me through; the waters were to the loins. Afterward he measured a thousand; and it was a river that I could not pass over: for the waters were risen, waters to swim in, a river that could not be passed over."*
>
> **Ezekiel 47:1-5**

How much of this river do you want? Are you going in ankle deep? Knee deep? Up to your waist? Or, are you going to get into the water that is deep enough to swim in? Stepping into God's river is a choice. God is not holding back His goodness and His glory from you. What are you willing to do, or stop doing, to be in the full flow of the river of God? During a move of God, there are some people that seem untouched by it. It is as if they are wearing spiritual raincoats. They just repel the rain of the Holy Ghost without being affected. I don't understand how that could be. Jesus will never be real to you until you get into the river.

"In the last day, that great day of the feast, Jesus stood and cried, saying, if any man thirst, let him come unto me, and drink. He that believeth on me, as the scripture hath said, out of his belly shall flow rivers of living water. But this spake he of the Spirit, which they that believe on him should receive: for the Holy Ghost was not yet given; because that Jesus was not yet glorified."

John 7:37-39

Jesus said those that would believe on Him, would have rivers flowing out of their innermost being. He did not say there would be a little trickle, but rivers. There should be a flow coming out of your inner man that produces life. The God kind of life, not a dead sea. It is a life-producing flow of the Holy Ghost. It is a river that will make a way where there seems to be no way. The river is going to go where people are hungry for God.

"There is a river, the streams whereof shall make glad the city of God."

Psalms 46:4

This river will touch every area of your life. When the river starts flowing in your life, you will be fulfilled. It is okay to relax and enjoy the journey. I like joy and gladness. I can only be sober for so long, then I need a release. Some people say they just don't understand about all this "revival stuff." You don't understand God or His move with your mind. It is a river that is flowing out of His Spirit. You just need to get in the river and things will change. It is like a slippery creek bank; if you hang out around this river long enough, you will eventually slip in.

Chapter 12

Fresh Oil

Some of you never got to experience churches of long ago; smaller churches out in the boondocks and in out of the way places. I can remember when I was in Bible college, I used to travel out to minister. Other young students and I would go into some churches where the pulpit looked as disorganized as a garage sale. There was always a bottle of olive oil close by that looked like it had been there for years. Sometimes we could not get the lid off of it because they had not used it in such a long time. When we finally got the thing uncorked, we wondered why we did! Rancid olive oil smells worse than castor oil.

So when it was time to pray for the sick, I would pull the cap off and put some oil on my finger, and I would almost go under the power myself. Not under the power of

God, but under the power of the stinky oil! You can obviously tell that it had been a LONG time since that church had fresh oil.

"...I shall be anointed with fresh oil."
Psalm 92:10

We need to have the fresh oil anointing of the Holy Spirit. There is a credit card company that tells us not to leave home without their card. You had better adopt that attitude regarding the anointing of the Holy Spirit! Don't leave home without it! Don't go away without that fresh touch of God in your life. It is the anointing that makes the difference.

One day I had to make a trip a few hundred miles out of town. I looked at my odometer and I realized that I was overdue for an oil change, so I took it in. I was reading my Bible in the waiting room of the garage while they were taking care of my car. The garage didn't have much business that day, so it was rather quiet. I had space and time to myself. As I was sitting there reading in Psalms 92 about fresh oil, it just leaped off the pages of God's Word. As I was looking at it, God was revealing something to me about the importance of fresh oil versus dirty oil.

Oil usually gets dirty before it wears out. Fresh oil is

cleansed from impurities. Fresh oil makes your car run cooler. It may cost more up front to change your oil and to use good quality oil, but it protects your investment. It will definitely pay off in the long run. I don't know about you, but not only do I have a lot invested in what I drive, but I have a lot invested in my personal walk with God. I have an investment in my marriage. I have an investment in my children and my grandchildren. I have an investment in my friends. I have learned that you either pay now or pay later. One way or another, it will cost you. If you invest in good quality oil changes now, you won't have to pay the auto mechanic a much larger sum later when your vehicle fails for lack of maintenance.

I will never forget a situation involving a staff member from many years ago. He had a beautiful gold-colored car. It was one of those long, two-door Lincolns. One day he called me from the repair shop of the Lincoln-Mercury dealership down the street from where our church was at that time. He said, "Pastor, I don't know what to do. My car is broken down. My engine is shot. They say that my oil is as thick as molasses. My car got hot and my engine froze. It only had 50,000 miles on it." I said, "Man, I can't even believe that! You have only 50,000 miles on it? How often do you change your oil?" He said, "Oh Pastor, I never change the oil, I just add oil." Being a rather frugal man, he would pick up whatever oil was on sale and just dump it in periodically. As long as it said "oil" on the can, it was okay by him. This man had a beautiful car with no reason in the world for it to go out. But his oil got hot and broke down and finally his engine just froze. At 50,000 miles, he had to trade it in and take a terrible loss. You pay now, or you pay later.

We have to get wiser. We need to be anointed with good quality, fresh oil. Any old oil will not do. I want the oil that works the best. I want the oil that I have faith in. I want the oil that has the best track record over a period of time. It is so important to maintain and take care of what you have. If you will take care of the investment God gave you, He will give you something bigger and better. I am talking about the anointing of the Holy Ghost.

Thank God that Psalms 92:10 applies to me and to you. "*I shall be anointed with fresh oil.*" I earnestly desire the touch, the anointing, the enabling, the empowering, the wisdom, the understanding, and the ability of the Holy Spirit of God more than anything on the face of this earth. This fresh oil anointing releases God to take care of our enemies.

"When the wicked spring as the grass, and when all the workers of iniquity do flourish; it is that they shall be destroyed for ever: But thou, Lord, art most high for evermore. For, lo, thine enemies, O Lord, for, lo, thine enemies shall perish; all the workers of iniquity shall be scattered."

Psalms 92:7-9

The worst thing you can do is to try to fight your enemies yourself. The best thing you can do is to forgive them, pray for them, and bless them. I did not say blast them; I said bless them. Just turn your enemies over to God. This fresh oil anointing of God releases God to take action on your behalf. When you really get in close to Jesus, you desire to be at peace with your enemies. When you get this fresh oil anointing, it is impossible to be full of hate, unforgiveness, and in strife with your enemies. It is impossible! This fresh oil releases Him to take care of our enemies.

This fresh oil anointing in us shows the goodness of God to those around us. We are living epistles. It's great to be around someone who is an encourager. They make you feel warmed and blessed. It causes you to want to spend more time around them. This fresh oil is *"to show that the Lord is upright"* (Psalms 92:15). I want my life to be an example of God's goodness. I want people to know that God is a good God. I want people to know that He is my Rock and there is no unrighteousness in Him. That is why I want to be filled with fresh oil. I want a regular, fresh infilling of the Holy Spirit of God.

"Neither is new wine put in old wine-skins; for if it is, the skins burst and are torn in pieces, and the wine is spilled and the skins are ruined. But new wine is

> *put into fresh wineskins, and so both are preserved."*
>
> **Matthew 9:17 (AMP)**

Maybe you were filled with fresh oil twenty years ago. That is great. The problem is that we tend to leak. That is why the Lord told us not to put new wine into old wineskins. The Bible said that if you put new wine into an old wineskin it will leak, it will crack, it will break and the wine will be lost. Pastors pour out the new wine of the Holy Ghost every Sunday morning and before some people get to the parking lot, they leak. Their wineskin breaks because it is not prepared.

We must prepare our wineskin so that when God pours out of His Spirit, it doesn't leak. Repentance and joy prepare your wineskin for revival. My prayer is, "Oh, God, give me a new wineskin. Prepare my heart to receive from you."

Is your wineskin prepared for the new wine? Has it become old and dry? If so, how can it be restored? There is an ancient process for the restoration of the wineskin. First, it had to be soaked in water for a period of time. After the wineskin softened up, it was sealed with oil. The oil was smeared all over it. The water represents the Word of God. We can get so crusty and dry. But when we come to church, we are soaking in the water of the Word. We need to sit and soak in the Word. The Word of God and the presence of God will soften us up. The oil represents the work of the Holy Ghost in our hearts. Once we are soft and pliable because of the washing and soaking of the Word of God, we are ready to be sealed by the oil of the Holy Ghost.

Once our wineskins are soft and pliable again, we are ready for the new wine. That brings me to what our church calls "carpet time." When we pray for someone and they are slain in the Spirit, we call that "carpet time." Why do we need "carpet time?" It is while we are down on the carpet that the oil and the wine are poured in. Since our wineskins are prepared and soft, the wineskin does not leak or break when God pours in the new wine. It lasts! It lasts even when you get home from church. It is there when you go to sleep and when you wake up the next morning. When our wineskins are restored, we can remain filled up.

In the early days of my ministry, every time I had to get in my car, I had to pray that I wouldn't run out of gas before I got to where I was going. I told myself that when things were better for me financially, I was going to always have gas in my car. Now, my car is filled with gas consistently. That is why my daughters have always loved driving my cars. I consistently have more gas than they do. Many times I would get into my car and realize that my daughters, Susan and Janet, had been driving it again. The gas tank was nearly empty. They liked to drive my cars and it showed.

Some people are out of gas before they leave the auditorium because they leak. They are always running on empty. By the time they get to their car, they do not even remember what the preacher preached. They have to look at their notes to figure it out. Not only does God want us to *get* full of the Holy Ghost, he wants us to *stay* full of the Holy Ghost. God wants us to sleep full of the Holy Ghost, to wake up in the morning full. He wants us to be full on our jobs. He wants us to be full so we can go out to a sick, negative, and dying world to tell them that there is more.

There is only one thing that can ultimately satisfy a man or woman of God, and that is the fresh oil of the Holy Ghost. I know it is the only thing that can satisfy me. Fresh oil has expanded my vision, it has rekindled the ministry that God has entrusted into my care, it has re-ignited our church, it has multiplied our harvest, and it has blessed our church financially. All of these things are great, but I know that I will continue to need fresh oil in order to keep revival flowing.

Chapter 13

What's
The Bottom Line?

I am thrilled to pastor a church where you can get saved on purpose! Today many churches will not even give an altar call. If they do say something about salvation, many times they will not even pray with people in front of the congregation. Jesus said in Matthew 10:32, *"Whosoever therefore shall confess me before men, him will I confess also before my Father which is in heaven."* I am not ashamed of the Gospel and I don't believe we should be ashamed to call sinners to repentance. If you are going to catch fish, you have got to bait the hook and go fishing!

People are ripe for salvation! Since the spirit of revival

began moving in our church, one area of noticeable increase has been our salvation altar calls. There were times in previous years that I could stand and beg people to come to Jesus and no one would respond. But something happened after we were touched by revival. The atmosphere in our church changed. Our hearts were stirred to bring in the lost. People invited their unsaved friends and family members to church because they knew there would be an altar call where they could be born again.

Today we have a sign on our podium for every minister to see. It reminds us to give a clear-cut, salvation altar call in every service. We never take an altar call for granted. God has honored our faith and now in almost every service, we see people respond to the altar call.

In our church we have a salvation altar call right after the praise and worship. I will never forget the Sunday morning when Kenneth Hagin was sitting on the platform and God told me to give the altar call right then. At first I wasn't sure about this because we had traditionally given the altar call following the message. I wondered if anyone would respond. About the third time God said it, I obeyed His voice. I walked up and gave the altar call and there was a landslide of souls that came forward. I learned a valuable lesson that day. I am not saying that everyone needs to do it that way and I cannot show chapter and verse that says we should. But I do recognize the voice of the Spirit. When we enter His presence through singing praise and worship, our hearts become tender and the Holy Spirit is free to do His work.

When an altar call is given, receive every person in God's love. Do not sit there and try to pick and choose. Don't try to figure out who should be there and who should not. Love them, pray for them, receive them and let God do a work of grace. Some people say, "Well, half of the people that respond to the altar call are just coming back to Jesus." What's wrong with that? Don't you want your friends and loved ones to be right with God? Thank God for people getting right and coming back to God. I rejoice for every person that comes to the Lord Jesus for the first time, but being a pastor, I also thank God when I see the fire of God re-ignited in people's lives.

When you talk about revival, you must remember that harvest is the bottom line. Paul wrote in Romans 10:1, *"Brethren, my heart's desire and prayer to God for Israel is, that they might be saved."* Paul was consumed with harvest. He wanted his people to be saved. That should be our passionate prayer every day of our life. It is my desire and prayer that my children, my grandchildren and ALL of my family be saved!

Revival brings a renewed desire to witness and see people born again. Be sensitive to the leading of the Holy Spirit and you will find yourself boldly witnessing. Early one morning my wife and I needed a few things, so I ran up to a convenience store near the house. I put on a hat to disguise myself because I looked like a mess. I was standing in the store and looked up to see one of the biggest slobs I had ever seen in my life. His beard was scraggly; he was quite a sight. He had just gotten his breakfast, a chili dog covered with onions. As he took it from the microwave, he took a bite and chili dribbled down the front of his shirt. I like chili and onions, but not at seven o'clock in the morning! There I was, Pastor Nichols, God's man of faith and power, born again, Spirit filled; yet completely appalled by the sight of this guy. I just wanted him to get out of the way so I could check out and go home.

While I was standing there like such a "spiritual person," God spoke to me. He told me to witness to that man. At first, I just stood there. He looked pretty mean. But God continued to speak to me about witnessing to him. I thought there was a chance that he would be gone by the time I checked out and maybe I wouldn't have to say anything. I tried to avoid it, but in my heart I knew what I had to do. As I was leaving, I saw the guy closing the door on his truck. Suddenly, I ran across the parking lot and leaped up on the running board of his truck and grabbed the driver's door. I said, "Sir!" He was just starting that old truck and he turned around and said, "YEAH?" By that time the anointing was flowing. I put my pride where it should have been all along. I began to tell the man about Jesus. He just looked at me. I did not get a commitment out of him, but I gave him the plan of salvation. When I got back in my car I was a different person than I was earlier at the checkout. I knew that God wanted the man to hear the gospel, but He also wanted to teach me something as well. We must reach out to the "undesirable." Revival should go beyond the four walls of our church. I want to see harvest!

Chapter 14

A Word to Leaders

Before revival hit our church, I was asking God to send a move of His Spirit. Although I desperately wanted revival, I was also wondering what we were going to do about all of our programs. A church of our size has so many things going on at once, it would be difficult to suspend all of these activities to accommodate revival. Revival seldom comes at man's convenience. What are we going to do about all the things we need to do? I bypassed my head and went with my heart.

Revival must take priority. Revival means that you, as a leader, may have to cancel things and rearrange your schedule. You may hurt your relatives' feelings because you miss an event, but your heart's cry must be, "However long it takes and whatever it takes, I am going to please God and I am going to see revival."

People told me that this "revival thing" could empty the church, but I knew we needed it. As a church, we had gone through hard financial times. Things had been getting better, but the struggle was taking its toll on me. If you live for a number of years with your back against the wall, you count your moves very carefully. But then something happened. There was a reckless abandon of the Holy Ghost that was released in my heart. I said, "God, whatever You want to do."

God made several transitions in our church. I believe with all my heart that the flow of revival that God wanted to bring could not have worked with the way things were in our church. God shuffled some things around. There were some things that had to be postponed. Some things had to be cancelled or phased out altogether. During that initial outpouring and for five months after, we had no youth services. When we started them up again they were stronger than before. The youth ministry had actually grown. The spirit of revival had hit Calvary Cathedral International and we would never be the same again. We are not perfect, but God has given us the anointing to do things that were not possible before. It is just awesome to see what God has done right across the board.

It is important who you have working along side of you. During that summer of revival, we were in the process of a business manager transition. I had almost made the final decision in favor of a man who was imminently qualified. He had a portfolio of qualifications that were astounding. I thought the man really had what we needed at that point. I said, "Hey, we are going to be in revival here for a week or two. We will pick up our talks when we get through."

The first time that he came to the meeting, he arrived late and left early. He came another time, arriving late and leaving early. It dawned on me as the revival went on for five weeks, that I had not seen him again. He had told me that he believed God wanted him to have the job. If he wanted the job as badly as he said, he would have been there. I said, "God, what am I going to do?" I looked down on the front row and I saw a man who was there at every service. He was happy and glad to be there. He was not there because he was on the payroll. He was weeping, shouting, leaping and praising God. He was there every time the doors were open. He has been on the front row ever since. God said, "That is your man right there." I thought, "Well Lord, I don't know about all his qualifications." But in my spirit I knew God was right. I still haven't heard from that other guy. I don't know what happened to him. I could have made a huge mistake. Under pressure, you will do some crazy things. Never make serious decisions under extreme pressure. Things can look so good when you are hurting so badly. You better pray going in, or you'll pray to get out!

So many pastors and ministers want to see church growth. The greatest way to have church growth is for a church to get full of the Holy Ghost. Many churches are cutting out church services because of lack of attendance. They are cutting back on their outreach programs. But thank God there are churches all over the world that are getting hungry for more of God. These churches realize that we do not need less, we need more—more of God. The writer of Hebrews said, *"Not forsaking the assembling of ourselves together, as the manner of some is; but exhorting one another: and so much the more, as ye see the day approaching."*

Someone said, "How are you handling all that laughter in your church?" I told them that happy people are a lot easier to pastor. They are wonderful people to pastor. I have pastored enough of those other kind. We need to allow people to flow in the manifestations of the Holy Ghost. Certainly, as leaders, we need to keep an eye on things. However, we need not throw the baby out with the bath water. I would rather manage a little wild fire than have no fire at all!

The fire of God has made a difference in our church finances. Nothing will get a preacher's attention any quicker than financial problems and we had our share of them before revival. During revival, our church finances just started going up. Calvary Cathedral has always paid its bills, but it was thirty days, sixty days, and sometimes even ninety days late. There were times we had to call creditors and ask for mercy. We would always catch up and it would always come in. Finances have increased thirty to thirty five percent since revival. After that initial outpouring in 1993, we finished in the black for the first time in our history! Every bill was paid and we started the year with a clean slate.

We have experienced the joy of the Lord in our church since revival came. The rejoicing can get pretty hilarious at times. As leaders, we need to sense when to keep our foot off the brake. We need to give our permission, so to speak, for people to celebrate. People need to be free to allow the Holy Spirit to flow through them.

A sad church has never won their world to the Lord. It is a happy church that will accomplish this. It is a joyful church. Blessed are they that know the joyful noise. We are not into noise for the sake of noise. We are not into gimmickry. We are into God. We are into the Holy Ghost. We are into seeing God meet peoples' needs.

I believe revival is the most important need in America and in the other nations of the world. We need righteousness in high places today. We need spiritual leaders to lead the way in revival. We need men and women of God who will carry this fire to every part of the globe. We need leaders who will pay the price and get the job done. I pray that God would raise up leadership who will walk in the power and the character of God!

If you are content with things the way they are, or if you can "make-do" with the current level of anointing in your church, you will stay there. But if you are hungry and you have an attitude of desperation—crying, "Oh God! I must have more!"—you will. I have seen God turn things around by His grace. Are you hungry for a move of God? If you are hungry, your people will get hungry.

Some leaders try to force revival by bringing in a well-known revival evangelist. That may be the worst thing that could ever happen. I tell pastors all the time, one of the greatest revivals that will ever happen in your church is when God sets your bush on fire. I'm talking about a burning bush experience with the living God. Let God set your bush on fire with the fires of revival. When you are in your home or church and they see your bush on fire, it will ignite their hearts too. Lasting revival will always be dependent on the pastor continuing to walk in revival.

When unwise preachers decide that they want revival in their churches, they tear their churches up by telling them how backslidden they are. Don't go to your congregation and beat them on the head and tell them how dead they are. Remember who killed them! Take the positive approach instead. Have you ever watched someone enjoying an ice-cream cone? Pretty soon it starts looking good. It makes you want one of your own. If you keep experiencing and enjoying revival they will want what you have.

There is a wonderful pastor from Canada who came to our ministers' conference and experienced a good deal of "carpet time." He got a revelation while he was on the floor under the power of the Holy Ghost. When he got up he said, "God, I see what this thing is all about." Do you know what that pastor did? He had his own personal revival. Then he called his staff in, and they had a personal revival. So first let personal revival blaze in your heart, then get the staff ablaze, then you are ready to approach the congregation with revival. In that church in Canada, you can walk into the auditorium before service times, and there are people walking around and praying boldly in the Spirit—boys and girls, teenagers, men and women. They don't need someone to stoke their fire; they are stirred up when they get there. They stir *themselves* up! You walk into their auditorium and it is like a blast from heaven. There is major revival up there now. Fires of revival are beginning to burn across different parts of Canada!

When Rodney Howard-Browne came to our church, he was like a bulldozer. Bulldozers have one gear meant to plow through everything. He did some bulldozing in our church. I looked around and a thought came to me. I knew immediately who planted the thought in my head. The devil said, "You are not going to have a church left." I said, "Well, we will just build it all over again."

You cannot be swayed by the lies of the devil or the fear

of man. There comes a time when you've got to do what you've got to do. There comes a time when you have to put your neck out and take the risk. There comes a time when you must become hungry enough for God, and you just have to get out there and do it.

Revival is fun, but it is work. People say, "Well, it is just wonderful. You are just out there having a great old time." It is wonderful, but I have to put my faith on the line for every meeting. My prayer is on the line. I am standing in faith believing. Just because there is a good preacher or a good singer, it does not mean you will automatically have revival. It requires faith.

One thing you will have to watch for in a move of God is offense. I have had some very good opportunities to be greatly offended. I am human and I have feelings too. I hurt too. I am sometimes tempted to carry the hurt for awhile. You know what I do, yes, an ordained pastor, I get down before God and say, "God, this does not really make a bit of difference at all. I humble myself before You. I would rather see revival than pet my flesh. I would rather see revival than receive an offense. I would rather see revival than worry about something that isn't going my way." You have to be prepared for the counter-attack. Offense is going to be one of Satan's main weapons in trying to stop the move of God.

Are you grasping that? I go through the same thing you go through. We all have to make a decision. Are we going to have God's best and refuse to be offended, or are we going to hinder the flow because of the spirit of offense?

Charles Finney said that any church can experience revival when it is willing and ready to pay the price. But it must start with the leadership. Once the fire is ignited and blazing in your life, then you can see it sweep through your church, your community, your city—it is limitless. Thank God for revival! If it is true that any church can experience revival, what are you waiting for? Go for it!

Chapter 15

Getting The Glory Back

In 1 Samuel 4:21 there is a terrible statement, *"the glory is departed from Israel."* You know the sad thing is, the glory could depart from many churches today and some would never know the difference. Many ministers have become too professional. They know how to stir people's emotions. Even if God did not show up, many preachers could carry on without Him. But there was a time, a sober time, when the glory of the Lord departed from Israel. I am crying out for America, "God do not let the glory of the Lord depart from this nation! Help us, Lord!" Oh we need God's glory!

When the rivers are not flowing and believers are oh so

dry, how do you get the river flowing again? How do you get the glory back? There are some beautiful instances in God's Word that can help us answer these questions.

"And it came to pass, when the priests were come out of the holy place: (for all the priests that were present were sanctified, and did not then wait by course: Also the Levites which were the singers, all of them of Asaph, of Heman, of Jeduthun, with their sons and their brethren, being arrayed in white linen, having cymbals and psalteries and harps, stood at the east end of the altar, and with them an hundred and twenty priests sounding with trumpets:) It came even to pass, as the trumpeters and singers were as one, to make one sound to be heard in praising and thanking the Lord; and when they lifted up their voice with the trumpets and cymbals and instruments of music, and praised the Lord, saying, For he is good; for his mercy endureth for ever: that then the house was filled with a cloud, even the house of the Lord; So that the priests could not stand to minister by reason of the cloud: for the glory of the Lord had filled the house of God."

2 Chronicles 5:11-14

As you can see in this passage it started with leadership. The priests came out of the holy place sanctified. "Sanctified" means separated for holy purposes. In 2 Corinthians 6:17, Paul wrote, *"Wherefore come out from among them, and be ye separate, saith the Lord, and touch not the unclean thing; and I will receive you."* Get your leaders lined up with the Word of God. Leaders need to take the lead in personal revival. Admitting that change needs to take place is an important step toward change. These same principles can be applied to the individual believer as well. Get rid of whatever has been hindering you from moving in revival.

Natural rivers like to follow the path of least resistance. There is a parallel here with the river of God. If you have strife or unforgiveness in your life, these become barriers or obstacles that hinder the flow. When people are in one accord and in divine order, it is so easy for the Holy Ghost to flow. The scripture records that on the day of Pentecost the people in the upper room were in one accord. To be in one accord means to have one passion. When the pastor and leadership agree that there must be revival, a major step has been taken. Revival must become a passion, not just an interest. With everyone on the same page, it will be much easier for turning things around.

I have been in churches where the staff was divided over revival. They were not in agreement and their body language showed it. Certain staff members would sit toward the back of the auditorium with their arms folded as if to say, "Just try and bless me." Unity and one accord is the atmosphere where revival can best take place.

Abraham spoke a classic word about leadership when he said to Lot, *"Let there be no strife,"* (Genesis 13:8). Strife does not work in a business, does not work in a home, does not work in a friendship, or in any relationship. Let there be no strife. We must flow together. There has to be harmony.

The priest came out of the holy place sanctified. That is the beginning point. Psalms 133:1-2 says, *"Behold, how good and how pleasant it is for brethren to dwell together in unity! It is like the precious ointment upon the head, that ran down upon the beard, even Aaron's beard: that went down to the skirts of his garments;"* This is the Biblical pattern. It starts at the top and comes down. When the church staff comes into agreement and seeks personal revival, then it will flow to the congregation. As the head goes, so goes the body.

"Then the trumpeters and the singers were as one, to make one sound, praising and thanking the Lord." Praising and thanking the Lord is something you can do every time you come to church, regardless of your circumstances. Maybe your week was rough, but thank God that after all you have gone through, He has brought you back one more time. It was when they lifted up their voice in one accord that things began to happen. This is so simple, yet so pow-

erful. You are not going to get everyone to praise the Lord every time, but you can get very close to it. If I were to say, "Let's all stand and give praise and thanksgiving to God." On the average, about eighty percent might do it. Let's get in agreement and let the Holy Spirit move. There is a harmony that brings the glory.

When people begin to worship God in spirit and in truth, God cannot resist responding to His children. When God responds, awesome things will happen. Our worship gets God's attention. I believe that God can only take so much. He can only take so much praise. He can only take so much giving before He just has to come and bless His people. Cornelius found this out (Acts 10). His prayers and alms had mounted up as a memorial before the Lord. I can just see that memorial rising up in heaven. It reached so high that every direction God looked, he could not help but see it. You can see the glory return if you keep praising. Keep talking revival. Keep singing about the move of God and the Holy Spirit. Rehearse the past moves of the Holy Ghost and be thankful to God for them. Keep pressing in. Continue to prepare for the next wave. Before long, you will see a breakthrough.

There are things that the Bible tells us we can do so that God cannot resist pouring out His power, His presence and His glory. One of the things we can do is to operate in a spirit of thanksgiving. God responds to a thankful heart. God just loves your voice. The Bible says in 2

Chronicles 5:13, *"as one, to make one sound to be heard in praising and thanking the Lord; and when they lifted up their voice in one accord..."* God loves to hear you giving thanksgiving and praise to Him. Everybody is a star with the Lord. Whether you can sing well or not, He loves to hear your voice. It does not make any difference if someone is watching me, I am just going to sing and praise God. I am going to praise him in the shower, in church, on the freeway; and I am not concerned with what anyone else thinks about it.

Being obedient will get the glory back. In the book of Acts, Jesus commanded the people to go to the Upper Room and tarry there until they were endued with power from on high. It does not take a brilliant person to understand that if He says "go and stay there," I had better go and stay there until something happens. I can choose to be obedient or I can do my own thing. I don't know about you, but every time I ever got into trouble, it was because I did my own thing. I am weary of my own thing. I want to do the will of God.

We must also recognize the importance of change. Have you experienced genuine change? Or are you still caught in the same old, same old—same old temper, same old bitterness, same old sarcasm, and same old gossip? Are you caught up in the same old spirits of offense? Change begins with the will. There must be a willingness on our part to humbly recognize that there is a need for change. If what we're doing is not working, we need to change. I am a different preacher than I was years ago, and I hope people can see the difference. As far as I was concerned, my wife did not seem like she needed any changes. But we have both changed. We have seen tremendous changes for the better in our lives and ministry as a result of revival.

If you are discouraged today because it seems like the glory has departed from your life, THERE IS HOPE! God responds to a genuine heart that is crying out for renewal. Be encouraged, stay hungry and you will see God's glory once again.

Chapter 16

The Secret
of Longevity

Occasionally, I enjoy getting in my car alone and driving to different areas in Fort Worth that remind me of the faithfulness of God. I drive past significant places in my personal history where God touched my life in a major way. Revisiting these places helps me to remember the roots of the ministry that God has entrusted to me. It gives me an opportunity to rehearse all of the great things that God has done in my life through the years. It helps to keep me thankful to God.

On one such occasion, I decided to drive over to the Old Stockyards area just north of downtown Fort Worth. I turned off of Main Street and drove up to a piece of property that had nothing on it but a slab of concrete. The area was now deserted. At one time, there was a large church building on that property. It was a thriving, vibrant church. People were being born again and filled with the Holy Ghost. It was one of the most alive churches in the city.

As I looked at that empty lot, I was taken back to a particular night where I had an experience with God in that very church as a 12 year-old boy. I had boarded a city bus that took me across town to the church. I remember that I was determined to meet with God that night. I was not leaving that place the same way I walked in. I sat through the service and at the end I went to the altar. I knelt and prayed and sought God with the innocence of a child. I was at the altar for quite some time. In fact, when I finally left, the only one remaining in the building besides myself was the janitor. That night was a defining night in my life. During that precious time at the altar, God filled me with the Holy Ghost. I am so thankful that at that crucial time in my life, I could go to a church that was alive with revival. It was a lifeline to me. Because of the move of God in that church, I was changed.

As I looked again at the vacant grounds where that great church had once stood, I thought about how important it is to have a church that is continuously in the midst of revival. There are so many people, young and old, who need to have access to a house where they can experience the tangible presence of God. They have so many needs that can only be met when they encounter the person of the Holy Ghost.

In my 40 years as the pastor of a church in the same city, I have seen many good churches come and go. I have witnessed many churches that were once sizzling with the fires of revival, either cool down or close down. The only explanation that I have for this is that somewhere along the way, these churches became stagnate. There was no change.

I have learned that you won't last if you don't change. One of the secrets of longevity is the willingness to change, even if it makes you uncomfortable. I am so thankful for what God has done in me and in our church in the past, but I cannot survive on yesterday's manna. I need fresh bread, fresh water, fresh oil. I have been called to be a pastor who carries and imparts to others the spirit of revival. It is why I was born. In John 18, when Jesus stood before Pilate, He was asked if He indeed was a king. Jesus answered in verse 37, *"To this end I was born, and for this cause came I into the world, that I should bear witness unto the truth."* Jesus knew his purpose. He knew what He was put on the earth to accomplish. God has given me a purpose. I am to proclaim to those who will hear, that we must hunger and thirst after God. We must remain in the spirit of revival.

I'm not willing to allow our church to be an artifact of revival history. We will not be a revival "has been." We will not be known only as the church that experienced a great revival in the past. My heart is crying out for present revival. Past revival can't meet our present needs. Hurting people need access to powerful, Holy Ghost churches that are relevant in our present world. Be thankful for the past move of God, but eagerly anticipate the new move of God. Wake up, church! Join me when I cry out at the top of my voice: "Oh God! Revive us again!"

Finney, Charles Grandison, *Lectures on Revival,* Bethany House, 1989.

Webster, Noah, *American Dictionary of the English Language,* New York: S. Converse, 1828.

Revival One-Liners

- Revival is in me.
- Revival is the moving of the third Person of the Trinity.
- Revival is restoration.
- Revival is change.
- Revival is seeing our need for God.
- Revival is turning around, going a different way and returning to God.
- Revival is like a cool drink of water when you are really thirsty.
- Revival is like a good meal when you are really hungry.
- Revival is like a good night's sleep when you are tired.
- Revival is change, repentance, new life and restoration.
- Revival is a greater love for God.
- Revival is falling in love with Jesus all over again.
- Revival is being filled with the Spirit.
- In real revival, things happen that some people have never seen before.
- In real revival, Jesus is the only star who receives all the glory.
- Revival always results in harvest.
- Real revival is a greater love for one another.
- Revival is a greater compassion for the sick and hurting.
- Revival is a greater mercy for those who have missed it or have fallen away.
- Revival is becoming more like Jesus.
- Revival is when people are convicted of their sins, forsake them and run after Jesus.
- Revival means being filled with the Holy Spirit and being more like Jesus in our daily walk, our business, and in our homes.
- Revival is purity.
- Revival is a fear of God.
- Revival is forgiveness.
- Revival will give you greater patience.
- Revival is outreach.

- Revival is getting involved in helping other people reach souls.
- Revival impacts your city.
- Revival gives people the desire to reach out with the gospel.
- Revival is a greater love for souls
- Revival is not a man or an evangelist.
- Revival is a Spirit.
- Revival is what God wants to say, when He wants to say it, the way He wants to say it.
- Real revival is not just about us.
- Revival will stir up a greater love for missions.
- Revival is hilarious, supernatural joy and gladness.
- Revival smokes out all the dead people.
- Real revival stirs up religious persecution.
- Revival is a greater love for your pastor.
- Revival is to be able to come and sit and say, "In the name of Jesus, I will hear what God wants me to hear."
- Revival will keep us in one accord.
- Revival is a greater love for giving of your tithes and offerings unto God.